History Insights

BRITAIN SINCE
1930

CONTENTS

Educational consultant: John Cook

Donna Bailey

BRITAIN AT WAR

People's lives have changed in many ways since 1930, but the single event to have the greatest effect on life in Britain was the Second World War.

Between 1939 and 1945 Britain was at war. We know a lot about how people lived during this period from diaries, newspapers, advertisements, photographs, letters, poems and films of the time.

At the beginning of the war, people thought the greatest danger would be from bombs dropped during air raids, and from poison gas attacks. Nearly 2 million air raid shelters were built, and everybody was given a gas mask which they had to carry all the time. A gas mask was hot and uncomfortable to wear, and in fact they were never needed.

People realised that the large cities and ports were the most likely places to be bombed, so plans were made to move or evacuate children to the countryside. In September 1939 3.5 million children were moved out of London and other big towns. Some very young children went with their mothers, but most children went alone, often not knowing where they were going. Each child wore a name tag and carried their luggage and a gas mask.

Some children enjoyed their stay away from home, but others hated it. They did not like living among strange people. Many children felt so homesick that they tried to run away. By Christmas 1939, half the children had returned home because the air raids had not yet started. Later on, when towns and cities were heavily bombed, children were once again sent to the country to escape danger.

During the war people had to cover their windows with blackout curtains at night, so that the German bombers would have difficulty finding their targets. Air raid wardens went around to check that no chink of light showed through the curtains. Car headlights were masked to cut down on the light, and there was a speed limit of 20 miles an hour in built up areas. Dashboard lights were not allowed, so drivers had to estimate their speeds and there were lots of accidents.

▲ *Children carrying their luggage and gas masks arrive in a strange town.*

▼ *People even slept in Underground stations during an air raid.*

Many thousands of people obtained air raid shelters in kit form and put them up in their gardens. At the sound of the first sirens warning of an air raid, people hurried into their shelters. In London people sheltered in the underground stations. After the 'All Clear' everybody came up again, often to find familiar streets a mass of rubble. Thousands of homes in Britain were destroyed in these bombing raids.

A major wartime problem was the shortage of food and other materials. Many ships importing food and other supplies were sunk by German submarines. Gradually scarce items such as petrol, food and clothes began to be rationed. Everybody was given a weekly ration book with coupons that could be exchanged for food or clothing.

Eggs were scarce and people were allowed one packet of dried eggs a month. The government issued recipes for making cakes without butter and sugar, and pies without meat and fruit. Magazines gave advice on how to use nettles to make tea, or dandelion leaves in salads. People were encouraged to grow their own food and to 'Dig for victory'. Children kept chickens in their back yards or on balconies, or rabbits which they fed on old cabbage leaves and carrot tops. People even joined pig clubs and fed their scraps to pigs.

▼ One person's weekly food ration.

▲ Posters urged people to 'Dig for Victory' and grow their own vegetables.

FASCINATING FACTS

A weekly food ration in 1941 for each person:

(1 oz = 28.35 g)

Meat	1 shilling 2 pence (6p) per week
Butter	2 oz
Cheese	1 oz
Tea	2 oz
Bacon or ham	4 oz
Sugar	8 oz
Cooking fats	8 oz

Fresh eggs and milk varied with the season.

HOUSES AND HOMES

Before 1930 there was a shortage of housing in Britain and many people lived in crowded Victorian slums.

In urban areas, many people lived in cramped flats or tiny 'bed-sits'. Country cottages and miners' houses often had outside toilets, no running water, and no baths.

During the 1930s many local councils built low-cost housing estates and re-housed people from the slums in rented 'council houses'. Council houses were all the same design, with small kitchens, inside toilets and bathrooms, three bedrooms and back-to-back gardens. At the same time, private companies built semi-detached houses and bungalows along main roads.

During World War II, air raids destroyed or damaged thousands of houses in towns and cities and made many people homeless. When the war ended housing was so scarce that 'squatters' often took over empty buildings. Emergency plans were made for prefabricated houses to be produced in factories.

▲ *Slum housing in Glasgow in 1960.*

❛ *There weren't no running water or inside toilets in our house, and no electricity in the village. The lavatory was a shed at the bottom of the garden, with a wooden seat and a pail underneath.* ❜

Fred Britten remembers his childhood home in the country in the 1940s.

◀ *A miner washes in a tin bath in 1934.*

4

City centres were reconstructed and new towns, such as Stevenage, Harlow and Peterlee were built, complete with new factories, schools, shops, and leisure facilities.

In the 1950s, more babies than usual were born and there was a huge demand for family houses. Councils began to build blocks of high-rise flats. These flats could be built quickly from prefabricated kits which were bolted together on site. Most councils put up these tower blocks to re-house people from the slum areas.

At first, many people were pleased with their new flats. They were modern and often had good views. However, their disadvantages were soon realised. Many tower blocks were badly built, they were expensive to heat, water often ran down the walls, the lifts regularly broke down and the passages and landings were dirty. People who were used to living in streets felt lonely shut up in their flats and there was nowhere for the children to play.

▲ 'Prefabs' were only meant to last for ten years but many people lived in them for much longer.

◄ A suburban living room in the 1950s.

After a gas explosion at Ronan Point in east London in 1968, people began to wonder if tower blocks were safe. It was discovered that many had been badly built. Some needed so much money spent on them that it was cheaper to blow them up. Most people preferred to live in new two or three-storey 'low-rise' flats, or in new or modernised semi-detached houses.

► Ronan Point after the gas explosion in 1968.

Just as houses have changed, so have the furniture and fittings inside them. In the 1950s, houses were cleaned with mops and sweepers. Floors were covered with shiny linoleum and mats. By the 1960s most households had a vacuum cleaner as well as a washing machine, refrigerator, telephone and television. Houses had wall-to-wall carpets, the walls and curtains were brighter and often in matching or contrasting colours. By the end of the 1970s most homes had central heating instead of coal fires or electric radiators.

A WOMAN'S PLACE

Before the war most women stayed at home and looked after the family.

Many houses had no electricity or running water and women spent much of their time keeping the house clean, washing clothes and cooking. During the war women spent long hours queuing for food and working out how to make their food rations go a little further. Advertisements in women's magazines reminded women to save fuel, mend clothes, and keep smiling.

So many people were needed to fight that in December 1941 women without children were called up to help the war effort. They could choose whether to go into the armed forces or to work in the factories. Some joined the Women's Land Army and worked on farms, while others made guns and shells in munitions factories. Other women drove ambulances, did voluntary work, ran canteens or took charge of anti-aircraft guns.

After the war most men expected women to return to being housewives, but many women wanted to carry on working. Most girls in the fifties were still only looking for a job until they got married and were not very interested in a career. However, the number of women going into higher education was slowly rising.

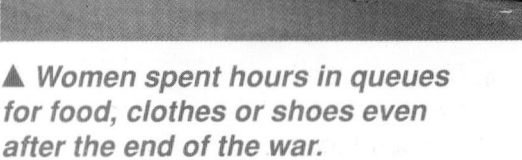

▲ A poster in 1941 urges women to become factory workers.

▲ Women spent hours in queues for food, clothes or shoes even after the end of the war.

◀ Women A.T.S. crew operate an anti-aircraft gun in Kent in 1942.

▲ *In the early 1950s most women stayed at home and looked after the house and family.*

❝*There's a feeling among the men at the moment that women must be in the factory solely because of the war but really women's place is in the home . . .*❞

From a Mass Observation Report of 1942

By the 1960s labour-saving devices in the home, such as improved cookers, washing-machines and vacuum cleaners, meant that women had more time to spare. Many women took part-time jobs in factories and offices, where they were paid lower wages than the men they worked with.

In 1970 the Equal Pay Act was passed so that women got 'the same pay for the same work'. Gradually a woman's wage became an important part of the family income, and women worked longer hours. But in many homes a woman was still expected to make the evening meal while her partner relaxed after a hard's day work.

In the late 1970s women began to apply for jobs that had previously been thought of as reserved for men. In 1975 the Sex Discrimination Act made it unlawful to advertise jobs for only male or female workers. More and more women began to have an independent career and the choice of whether and when they wanted to be married or have children.

▼ *Demonstrators campaigning for Women's Rights in the 1970s.*

◀ *Office workers in the 1960s. Notice the manual typewriters and old-fashioned telephone.*

FASCINATING FACTS

In 1951 only one married woman in five was in employment. By 1981 the figure had risen to three in five. Over half of these women were employed part-time.

THE CHANGING WORKPLACE

During the early 1930s there was a worldwide economic crisis, known as 'The Great Depression'.

This caused mass unemployment in Britain throughout the 1930s. Coal mines in South Wales closed, and when the shipyard at Jarrow closed in 1936, so many people lost their jobs that the workers marched to London to protest against high local unemployment and poverty. This march, known as 'the Jarrow hunger march', helped to start new industries in the area and elsewhere.

During the war, industry boomed. Factories were busy making the goods needed to fight. Aircraft came off the production lines at the rate of about one an hour. Munitions factories made guns, shells and bullets, and shipyards made new ships to replace those that had been sunk.

When the war ended in 1945, Britain needed money to rebuild cities and ports, to house homeless people and to pay off the money borrowed from other countries. Shortages and rationing continued while tremendous efforts went into making cars, ships and goods to sell to other countries. The government nationalised (took over) the coal, iron and steel industries and installed much needed new machinery. Electricity and gas, the railways and airlines were also nationalised. All these industries provided many people with jobs and money to spend.

By the late 1950s Britain had recovered from the effects of the war. Rationing finished in 1954, and many people were now able to buy cars, refrigerators and televisions sets for the first time.

▲ Unemployed workers pass through Harrogate during their 300-mile walk from Jarrow to London in 1936.

By the 1970s the traditional 'heavy industries' of shipbuilding, coal, iron and steel were suffering from competition from abroad. Jobs were lost as textile factories, shipyards and steelworks closed down and unemployment began to increase.

Many people found jobs in the new industries. Oil from the North Sea was first brought ashore in 1975. The production of North Sea oil and gas provided jobs for people building and working on oil rigs. It also gave work to those supplying the materials and services needed to support the oil rigs.

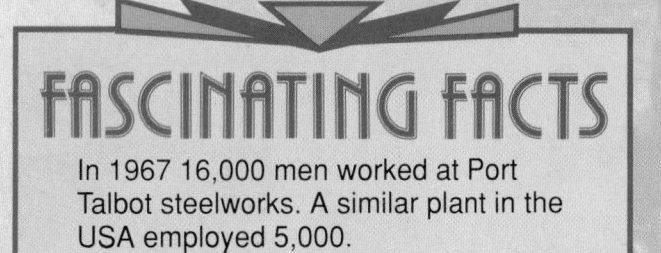

FASCINATING FACTS

In 1967 16,000 men worked at Port Talbot steelworks. A similar plant in the USA employed 5,000.

▲*The coal industry was nationalised in 1946, but the winter of 1947 was very cold and coal stocks ran out.*

▲ *A modern North Sea oil rig.*

Service industries such as banking, insurance, shops and tourism provided more new jobs. In manufacturing, the new electronic and chemical industries became more important than the old heavy industries.

New technology has produced products, such as video-recorders and calculators, that have changed everyone's lives. Computers have changed the way we live and work.

◀ *Interior of the Morris factory in 1960.*

COMING AND GOING

People are continually leaving Britain to live in other countries (emigrating), while others enter Britain to set up permanent residence (immigrating).

People move to other lands to escape from wars, from hunger and poverty, or to find a better job and a better life.

After the war, many British people felt they would be better off in Australia, New Zealand or Canada. Thousands decided to take advantage of the cheap fares that were offered to emigrants to Australia. Others went to South Africa and Rhodesia (now Zimbabwe).

During World War II many people came to Britain. From early 1942 American troops, known as GIs, began to arrive to help win the war. The disasters of war and persecution in Europe led to the arrival of large numbers of Jews, Poles, Greek Cypriots and Spaniards, while other people came seeking work. Many thousands of West Indian workers joined the war effort in the shipbuilding yards and munitions factories, as well as in the forces.

▶ **Many foods, like this mango, are now available in British shops.**

After the war, Britain desperately needed more workers, and people from the West Indies responded to advertisements for staff by London Transport. Asian doctors and nurses were recruited by the National Health Service. In June 1948, 492 Jamaicans came to Britain on board the *Empire Windrush*. By 1958 about 125,000 West Indians had come to live in Britain. At the same time people from India and Pakistan came to settle in Britain. Many employers lent their new staff the fare to Britain which they later repaid out of their wages.

▼ **Hungarian refugees who arrived in Britain in 1956.**

▲ **West Indian immigrants arrive at Victoria station, London in June 1956.**

Many of the new settlers had difficulties in finding homes in the post-war housing shortage and had to live in flats and bed-sits. Many people coming from Asia had the added difficulty of not speaking much English. Some groups found it easier to live together in communities. New arrivals encountered discrimination in many forms. Often, despite having many skills, they were turned down for jobs because of the colour of their skin. The Race Relations Acts of 1975 and 1978 made it illegal to make racial discriminations in housing, employment and education.

FASCINATING FACTS

In most years since 1948 more people have left than entered Britain.

▼ *The Notting Hill Carnival, held in London each year, is a dramatic celebration of African and Caribbean cultures.*

❝I was turned down for all the posts that I applied for. It was quite usual then for employers to say 'No thanks, we don't want blacks here'. In the end I had to take work on the night shift in a car factory, doing a very dirty job, for which I was paid very little.❞

From *Family in the Sixties* by Alison Hurst, describing the experiences of Sukhminder Bhurji, a science graduate, when he first arrived in Britain.

▲ *A family discusses migration to Australia with an official at Australia House.*

► *The Chinese New Year is celebrated in London each year.*

NEW IDEAS AND VALUES

During this century Britain has become a multicultural society.

Up until the 1950s, most people in Britain who were religious followed the Christian faith, and went to church on Sundays. However, now the British population is made up of various different cultures and people are free to worship in their different traditions, whether Christian, Muslim, Sikh, Hindu, Jew or Buddhist. Each has its own customs and ceremonies.

CHRISTIANS

Christians follow the example and teachings of Jesus. The most important thing for Christians is to love God and to care for other people. They study the Bible and celebrate many festivals linked with the life of Jesus, such as Christmas, Shrove Tuesday, Good Friday and Easter. There are different Christian groups who worship in their own way, including Roman Catholic, Eastern Orthodox and Protestant.

BUDDHISTS

Buddhists follow the teachings of Buddha. They try to avoid harming any living thing, to promote happiness and to help people to overcome suffering.

JEWS

The Jewish religion is called Judaism. Jews believe there is one God and that the Jewish people were chosen by God to obey his will.

MUSLIMS

The Muslim religion is called Islam. Muslims believe that there is one God whom they call Allah, and that Mohammed is his prophet.

HINDUS

Hinduism is the name people give to the many religious beliefs and customs that come from India. One of its central ideas is reincarnation.

SIKHS

The Sikh religion comes from Northern India. In the Sikh community everyone is equal, and they share food together after worship.

▲ *Children act out a nativity play to celebrate the story of the birth of Jesus.*

▶ *A Hindu prays to the gods.*

12

▲ *A mosque used by Muslims for worship in Woking, Surrey.*

▲ *The Sikh Golden Temple in Amritsar India.*

FASCINATING FACTS

Christians, Jews and Muslims share many of the stories and traditions that are told in the Bible. They share some of the same prophets, such as Noah, Abraham and Moses, and have the same holy city, Jerusalem.

▼ *A service underway inside a Jewish synagogue.*

▼ *A Buddhist Peace Pagoda in Battersea Park, London.*

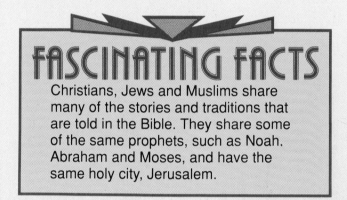

NEW SCHOOLS FOR OLD

In 1938 children started school at the age of five and left school at the age of fourteen.

Around 37 per cent of pupils stayed at the same school for their whole education in the late 1930s. All other children left their elementary (primary) school at the age of 11 and either went to a fee-paying grammar school or to a secondary modern school.

During the war 5,000 schools were damaged by air raids. There was a shortage of teachers, books and paper, and classrooms were crowded, sometimes with over 50 children in one class. After the war, the school-leaving age was raised to 15 and there was an urgent need for new school buildings. Many new secondary schools were built. Primary school children were often taught in huts built on bomb sites or playgrounds, or in Victorian buildings with small windows and enclosed playgrounds.

◀ *During the war, school lessons were held in some very strange places, such as in stately homes.*

After 1944, secondary education was free. At the age of 11, children took the 11-plus exam to see whether they should go to a grammar school or to a secondary modern school. Children in secondary modern schools learned the basic skills of Maths and English, with lots of time spent on practical subjects. Grammar schools prepared pupils for examinations that would allow them to go on to university.

Before 1950 children learned by memorising and chanting out facts. Children sat in rows at their desks and had to be quiet and obedient in class. They were not expected to ask questions or to interrupt the teacher.

During the 1960s some primary teachers began to teach in a less formal way so that children could learn at their own pace. Children sat in groups at tables to work at different activities.

Some people in the 1950s were worried that secondary modern schools were not very good. Children often felt they were failures if they did not pass their 11-plus exam. In the late sixties and early seventies parents began to send their children to comprehensive schools.

▼ *The playground of an old primary school in 1971.*

▶ *Primary school children had a free bottle of milk during the break until the 1970s.*

These took pupils of all abilities, and there was no need to take the 11-plus. The school-leaving age was raised to 16 in 1972. By 1980 nearly all secondary schools in England and Wales were comprehensive. Only a few places still had grammar schools. The remaining children went to public schools where their parents paid fees for their education.

❝*When I was at school, we each sat at a one piece wooden desk with an inkwell in the top. The ink monitor filled up the inkwells and we wrote with steel pen-nibs fixed to wooden handles. You dipped the nib into the inkwell every two or three minutes, and tried not to leave blots of ink on the paper, or you got a bad mark. I was very proud of my first fountain pen, which was much easier to write with – there were no ballpoints or biros in those days.*❞

Veronica Bonar remembers school in the 1950s.

◀ *Kidbrooke School, London, the first comprehensive school, was a purpose built school which opened in 1954.*

FASCINATING FACTS

In 1957 School Broadcasting started in Britain.

SHOPS AND SHOPPING

Pre-war town centres and high streets looked very different from the way they look today.

Large towns had department stores which sold goods in different areas, or departments, of the same shop. Most other shops were quite small and were owned by individuals. Shop assistants served people from behind the counter, weighing out things such as rice, flour or dried fruit for each customer. Specialist shops, such as a fishmonger, haberdasher or florist, only sold one kind of product. Small corner shops carried a whole range of goods. Few people owned a refrigerator, so people went to their corner shop three or four times a week.

During and after the war, when food was rationed, shopping habits changed. Meat was scarce and some people even bought horse meat, which did not need the usual coupons.

In the 1950s chain stores such as Woolworths and Marks and Spencer's opened large new shops in town centres. Self-service supermarkets began to replace the corner shops. Food was sold in packets and tins, and people could take what they wanted from the shelves and pay at check-out desks. In the 1960s, shopping at supermarkets became a weekly rather than a daily excursion. Many supermarkets offered shopping stamps such as Green Shield stamps, to persuade people to buy from them rather than shop in a rival store. People were given stamps according to how much money they spent, and could then exchange the stamps for gifts from a catalogue.

▲ *A village grocery in the 1950s.*

▼ *In 1949 there was such a shortage of fresh meat that people ate horse meat.*

▲ *Some supermarkets tried to encourage shoppers with Green Shield stamps.*

In 1971, the old pounds, shillings and pence were replaced by a new decimal currency.

New kinds of foods appeared on supermarket shelves, such as ready-to-eat meals, frozen foods, or dried packet meals. Vegetables and fruit could now be bought out of their growing season. New kinds of fruits and vegetables from other countries appeared. Foreign holidays gave people the taste for different foods, Asian immigrants introduced new spices to the kitchen, and West Indians brought over new vegetables such as sweet potatoes and okra.

> 6'When you went to Sainsbury's you went to the bacon counter, and he took the bacon off the hook and carved it for you. He took the butter off a great big block about 20 inches by 20 inches and he used to cut a block off and pat it with the wooden butter boards and pack it up in paper. At the grocer all his dried goods would be in sacks in front of the counter and he would fill your bags.9

Edna Sims remembers shopping before the Second World War.

▼ *A supermarket in 1971 at the time of the change over to decimal currency.*

▼ **Woolworths in the 1950s was a very busy chain store.**

The 1970s saw another change in shopping habits with the building of shopping centres and out-of-town hypermarkets. These provided convenient car parking and a whole range of goods under one roof. Some towns closed off their centres to provide a traffic-free area for shoppers.

Many small local shops were unable to compete with the low prices of the chain stores and supermarkets and closed down. High streets all over Britain began to look the same.

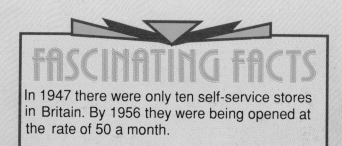

FASCINATING FACTS

In 1947 there were only ten self-service stores in Britain. By 1956 they were being opened at the rate of 50 a month.

WASTE NOT WANT NOT

During the war everything was in short supply and people did not waste as much as they do today.

Bits of string were carefully saved and tied up, lights were turned off to save energy, slivers of soap were moulded together, clothes were mended and old woollen jumpers unpicked to be knitted up again. No food was wasted, and children had to finish up everything on their plates. Any scraps or leftovers were used to feed chickens or pigs. Saucepan mountains appeared in 1940 when people responded to appeals for aluminium utensils which could be turned into planes. Even railings were torn down to make scrap iron for the war effort.

When the war was over, people were not so careful about waste. After all the shortages, it was a pleasure to buy new goods rather than re-use old things. People were encouraged to spend rather than save. Supermarkets introduced pre-packaged goods, and all the bottles and cans, paper and plastic were simply thrown away.

▼ *It was said that 2000 aluminium saucepans would make one aeroplane.*

At the same time people began to want more eggs and chickens, pigs and vegetables. To satisfy this growing demand, farmers reared chickens in battery cages, and pigs were kept in small pens. Vegetables were grown using fertilizers and pesticides, without thinking about the damage these chemicals do to the environment. The modern method of farming with huge machines meant that hedgerows were ripped up and the habitats of many birds and animals were destroyed.

In the 1950s, London was famous for its 'pea-soup' smogs caused by the smoke from thousands of coal fires. In 1952, the smog caused many deaths in London. In 1956 the government passed the Clean Air Act, which forced people to burn smokeless fuel in their grates, and controlled the gases given out by industrial plants. Gradually the smog disappeared.

▼ *Factory smoke pollutes the air, and industrial waste fouls the river and poisons the waters.*

▼ *On 1 April 1967 the huge oil tanker Torrey Canyon was wrecked off the coast of Cornwall. Thousands of tons of oil spilled into the sea, and spread along the coast, killing fish and seabirds.*

In the 1960s people began to see how the environment was being threatened by their way of life.

In the early 1970s many conservation societies, such as Greenpeace and Friends of the Earth, were started. They recognised the threats to the environment caused by pollution and acid rain. Scientists said that fossil fuels such as coal, oil and gas would run out before the next century, and renewable forms of energy such as wind and solar energy were developed. People became aware of the problems of waste disposal, litter and pollution, and the word 'recycling' became part of the language. Bottle banks and recycling paper bins were set up in towns, and motorists were encouraged to use lead-free petrol.

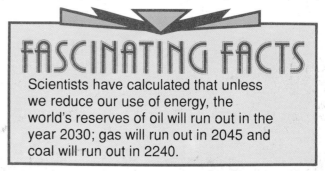

FASCINATING FACTS

Scientists have calculated that unless we reduce our use of energy, the world's reserves of oil will run out in the year 2030; gas will run out in 2045 and coal will run out in 2240.

19

THE RAG TRADE

Before the war, most new and fashionable clothes were made by dressmakers or tailors, or made at home on sewing machines.

During the 1930s, department and chain stores such as Marks and Spencer's and C & A sold cheap factory-made clothes made from rayon, an artificial fibre.

During the war clothes were cheap and hard-wearing, in simple, practical styles. Some people made clothes from curtain material, parachute silk or even grey army blankets. Children wore clothes made from their parents' old garments. Women began to wear trousers, known as 'slacks'. One advantage of trousers was that they made stockings, which were hard to find, unnecessary.

After the war there was an immediate reaction to the dull, uniform look of wartime fashion.

Men's clothes during the 1930s were stiff and awkward. Businessmen wore shirts with stiff collars, waistcoats and thick suits, even in summer. Working men wore rough trousers, a jacket and a flat cap, although most struggled to own a best Sunday suit and a bowler hat.

In the 1950s tweed jackets and flannel trousers became popular for casual wear. Men's fashions were also influenced by film and pop stars, such as Marlon Brando and Elvis Presley. Boys began to copy Brandon's style of leather jackets and tight trousers.

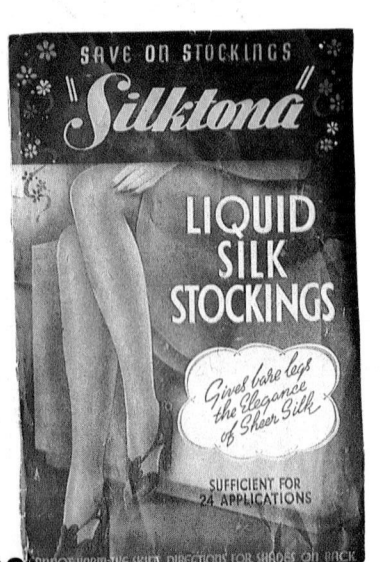

◄ During the war stockings were hard to get hold of, and many women painted on liquid stockings.

▼ *In 1947 the 'New Look' introduced softly rounded shoulders, small waists and long, swirling skirts. New materials such as nylon, lycra and PVC allowed ordinary people to copy the fashions of the day.*

► *In the 1950s girls' skirts were held out with layers of petticoats.*

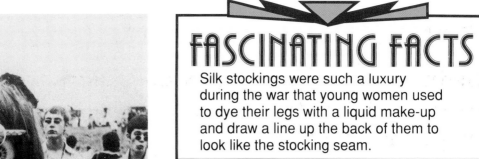

Silk stockings were such a luxury during the war that young women used to dye their legs with a liquid make-up and draw a line up the back of them to look like the stocking seam.

◀ *In the late 1960s, Hippies wore ethnic styles with long skirts, scarves, beads and light cotton materials.*

EVENING STAND

IRA CHIEFS I
IN YARD SWO

Evening Standard
EVENING NEWS
ON SALE HERE

▶ *Boys who took to wearing 'Edwardian' style clothes in the 1950s were nicknamed 'teddy' boys. They wore narrow string ties, knee-length jackets, narrow 'drainpipe' trousers and thick crepe-soled shoes.*

▲ *Bright coloured trouser suits made from synthetic material were popular in the 1970s.*

FROM WALTZ TO DISCO

Since 1930, music and dance styles have changed dramatically.

Before the war many people enjoyed ballroom dancing. They went to dance halls where they often danced the waltz, the quickstep and the foxtrot. The arrival of the American troops, with their big bands and their catchy rhythms, had a tremendous effect. Young people forgot about the waltz and the foxtrot. Instead jiving and jitterbugging were all the rage. At the same time, people enjoyed songs sung by Vera Lynn, who was nick-named 'The Forces Sweetheart'.

In the 1950s the big bands continued to be popular and housewives tuned in their radios to hear crooners like Bing Crosby, Frank Sinatra or Perry Como singing love songs. But things changed overnight when Bill Haley's single *Rock Around the Clock* went to No 1 in November 1955. A new rhythm and sound were introduced to popular music – 'rock and roll' was born. Soon stars such as Elvis Presley and Buddy Holly rose to the top of the charts. On Saturday nights, clubs and dance halls were filled with teenagers dancing to the pounding rhythms of rock and roll. Jazz also remained popular, and young people listened to their favourite songs on a juke box in the nearest coffee bar.

Until the 1960s, American music and musicians were at the top of the pop charts. Then, in 1963 a group from Liverpool, The Beatles, leapt to the top of the charts with *From Me To You*, the first of 11 consecutive No 1s. Soon pop charts all over the world were full of records from British groups like the Rolling Stones, The Who, and The Shadows. Young people bought cheap vinyl singles, which were played so often on radio and television that the performers became household names. Teenagers tuned in to listen to the illegal 'pirate' radio stations like Radio Caroline on the North Sea.

▲ *Ballroom dancing in 1954.*

► *Juke boxes played the latest music.*

FASCINATING FACTS

Over 300 pop groups formed in Liverpool during the 1960s.

▲ *Elvis Presley, rock 'n roll's greatest star, during the filming of* Love me Tender *(1956).*

The first discothèque opened in 1961. Unlike at a traditional dance hall, people danced to records played by a DJ rather than to live music. In 1969 many pop fans flocked to the Isle of Wight for one of the first major British pop festivals, where singers such as Bob Dylan and Jimi Hendrix played, as well as many famous British pop stars.

In the early 1970s disco music and glam rock become fashionable. In the late 1970s punk rock leapt into the news. It was aggressive and voiced the anger of the youth of the day. Groups such as the Sex Pistols and The Clash were very popular.

▲ *During the 1960s the Beatles caught the attention of the young, and started a craze called 'Beatle Mania'.*

▲ *Let's twist again – the popular dance of the 1960s.*

▶ *Jimi Hendrix helped change the style of guitar playing in the 1960s.*

GETTING AROUND

Transport and travel has changed a lot since the 1930s.

Before the war few people could afford cars. Rail travel was cheap and the railways ran trains which stopped at even the smallest of rural stations. During the war, the railways were organised by the government and in 1947 they were nationalised. During the 1950s passengers gradually began to stop going by train as people bought their own cars.

In 1963 the railway chief, Dr Beeching, recommended that about a third of all railway lines should be closed. The drift away from rail travel continued, in spite of the new high speed intercity trains introduced in 1976. Today, railways carry less then ten per cent of the travelling population.

The decline of the railways was mainly due to the increasing number of private cars. In the 1930s Britain had the second largest motor industry in the world, but few people could afford to buy a new car. Most people went to work by bus or bicycle. During the war, petrol was rationed, and factories stopped making cars to make planes and tanks. After the war, the motor industry started up again. Cars were now more comfortable, faster and more economical on petrol, and many people bought their own cars. Young people in the fifties bought mopeds and scooters. In 1959 the Mini first appeared in car showrooms. It was cheap and easy to drive and became very popular, especially with young drivers.

▼ *As the number of cars on the road increased, membership of the AA grew.*

> ❝*I bought my first car in 1958 for £65. It was a red MG and was already 25 years old then. It had a top speed of 60 miles an hour going downhill. When it didn't start I had to turn the engine over with a starting handle, rather like a huge key.*❞

George Bailey remembers.

▲ *Alec Issigonis designed the Mini in 1959.*

▶ *Each tiny village or town had its own railway station in the 1950s.*

24

More cars on the roads meant more traffic problems, delays and hold-ups. The first motorway was opened in 1958. Bridges over the Forth (1964), the Severn (1966) and the Humber (1981) shortened journey times, and by-passes ended the traffic jams in town centres. The number of people killed in road accidents increased, so speed limits were introduced in 1967 to cut down on the rate of accidents. At the same time police used breathalyser tests to cut down on the number of drunken drivers.

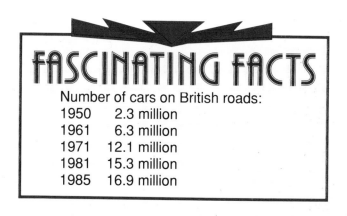

▲ Motorways meant that journey times were much shorter, but the motorways themselves soon became blocked by traffic.

Owning a car meant that people had more freedom to travel when and where they wanted, for outings and holidays. At the same time more people began to travel by air. Before the war, Britain's Imperial Airways carried passengers to Australia and South Africa in flying boats which took off and landed on water. The planes, which could carry only 38 passengers, had to stop on the way to refuel.

▶ Concorde, the world's first supersonic aircraft.

During the war, aircraft design improved, but it was not until 1952 that the world's first jet airliner, the Comet, flew with BOAC (British Overseas Airways Corporation). Jet airliners encouraged more people to travel by air. To cope with the increased traffic, planes were lengthened so that more passengers could be fitted in. In the 1960s even larger aircraft, Boeing 747s, called Jumbo jets, were built. They could carry up to 500 passengers.

In 1969 Concorde, the first supersonic (faster-than the speed of sound) airliner entered service. Concorde can carry up to 144 passengers at twice the speed of sound and can cross the Atlantic in three hours. Today nearly all long distance international travel is by air.

▼ The introduction of the Intercity 125 has cut travel times enormously.

LEISURE AND PLEASURE

Since the 1930s, leisure has developed into an enormous industry.

Before the 1930s, few people had an annual holiday. But gradually more and more factories closed down for a week in the summer and holiday became a part of working-class life. Railway companies offered special holiday fares and many families went to the seaside for their annual holidays. People stayed in boarding houses or at holiday camps, such as Butlins and Pontins, which provided organised games and activities.

Some families preferred to go walking and hiking. Youth hostels provided cheap accommodation for walkers and cyclists. Sports such as golf, tennis and cricket were enormously popular, and crowds of people turned out to watch their sporting heroes.

GREETINGS— BING CROSBY

GREETINGS— DORIS DAY COLUMBIA RECORDS PUBLISHED BY MOVIE STAR SERVICE

▲ *Stars of the stage and screen became increasingly popular during the 1950s.*

In 1952 airlines introduced the first 'tourist' fares, and more people began to take holidays abroad. Young people began to hitch-hike both in Britain and on the Continent.

At home, many young people in the fifties joined youth clubs, while others met in jazz clubs and coffee bars. Younger children went regularly to the cinema on Saturday mornings to watch children's films about cowboys, space adventures and cartoons.

During the 1960s, most young people owned a record player, a stack of black vinyl records and a transistor radio. The craze for ten pin bowling started in 1960. Soon many towns in Britain had bowling alleys, but the craze did not last long. More people began to travel abroad on package tours arranged by travel companies. Larger cross-Channel ferries came into service.

▲ *Bobby Moore, captain of the 1966 England team that won the World Cup after a 4-2 victory against West Germany.*

People now took their cars and caravans on holidays abroad, while cheap trans-Atlantic fares opened up the possibility of holidays in the United States and Canada. Football became very popular as more and more people bought television sets and could watch live matches at home. Wildlife parks became a popular weekend or holiday excursion.

New sports appeared in the 1970s. The craze for skateboarding started, and for jogging. For those who could afford it, hang gliding, canoeing and skiing offered excitement and danger. Marathons became very popular with serious runners. People who wanted a more gentle form of exercise took up yoga. Violence at football grounds led to more people watching the sport on television rather than going to matches.

▲ *This picture shows many of the things popular with teenagers in the 1950s.*

▼ *A traditional seaside holiday, Margate beach 1955.*

A SHRINKING WORLD

Radio and television are now so much a part of everyday lives that it is difficult to imagine a world without them.

In the 1930s, 75 per cent of households owned a radio, or wireless as it was called then.

During the war the radio was used by both sides to broadcast misleading propaganda messages to the enemy. People in Britain were eager to hear the latest news of victories or defeats, and were encouraged by the speeches made by their leaders, especially by Winston Churchill. People in other countries listened to the BBC foreign service for news. Coded messages were broadcast for agents working in enemy territory. During and after the war, going to the cinema was a weekly event for many people. The most popular films were the British war films or American romances and musicals. Small news theatres showed news reels of world events.

▼ *During the 1930s the radio was an important form of entertainment.*

In the early 1950s only a few families owned television sets. These had small black and white screens and the BBC only broadcast a limited number of programmes each day. Many people bought their first television in 1953 to watch the Queen's coronation. When independent television started to broadcast popular programmes such as quiz shows and serials, there was an enormous rush to buy sets. By the end of the 1950s most homes had a television set, although it was not until 1967 that colour sets were available.

Cinema audiences fell off rapidly with the spread of television and many cinemas closed down. Television also affected the numbers of people going to sporting events and to theatres. However, people began to borrow more library books, perhaps because viewers were discovering new areas of interest. Books now started to be printed in colour with lots of pictures, and Sunday newspapers began to produce colour supplements.

As older people switched from radio to television, programmers saw young people as the new radio audience. 'Pirate' radio stations, such as Radio Caroline and Radio Luxemburg, began to broadcast non-stop programmes of pop music. Most pirate radio stations closed down after the BBC reorganised in 1967 and introduced Radios One, Two and Three.

During the 1960s, one of the most popular TV programmes was *That Was The Week that Was* which made fun of individuals or organisations such as the government, the church, the army or the Royal Family.

Documentaries, such as *Cathy Come Home,* made people aware of social problems. People could watch events as they took place, such as the moon landing in 1969 of Neil Armstrong and Buzz Aldrin. Many of today's popular television programmes began in the 1960s. For example *Coronation Street*, *This is Your Life*, *Top of the Pops*, *Blue Peter*, *Thunderbirds*, *Dr Who*, and *Dad's Army*.

6 *In the 1930s always on a Saturday we went to the Central Hall in Ilford to attend the cinema there where we had a woman pianist supplying the background music to the black-and-white silent film. This cost us 2d and for that 2d we also had an orange and nuts given free as part of our entrance fee.*9

Alec Clarke remembers.

▼ *A family watches television in the early 1950s.*

▲ **Many people bought TV sets to watch the Queen's coronation in 1953.**

INVENTIONS AND DISCOVERIES

Many of the things that we take for granted today were unknown before the war.

During the war enormous advances were made in scientific and medical research. Scientists developed radar (Radio Detection and Ranging) which made it possible to detect enemy ships and planes. Microwaves, short radio waves, were developed from the work on radar. Microwaves were first used to carry black and white television signals. Today they carry many television programmes, now in colour, and many telephone circuits. They are also used for cooking.

▲ *Early computers took up a lot of space, such as this one, built at Manchester University in 1949, and hailed as 'a marvel of our time'.*

During the war, the Germans launched V2 rockets against cities in Britain. The V2 led to the development of multi-stage rockets later used to launch satellites into space. In 1962 Telstar, the world's first communications satellite was launched. Communication satellites are used to send television, telephone and computer signals around the world. Weather satellites provide weather forecasts, and observation satellites provide valuable information about earth's resources and help in pin-pointing such things as forest fires, crop diseases and oil slicks.

Radio waves are only one way of carrying messages. In 1966 scientists suggested that tiny strands of very pure glass called optical fibres could be used to carry short bursts or pulses of light. Lasers are used to send messages down optical fibres, and to 'read' bar codes in supermarkets, play compact discs, and in surgery.

▼ *The microchip has led to the development of compact computers.*

Lasers are used to control light signals, but electronic circuits are used to control the flow of electricity. Before the war, radios used fragile electronic valves to control and change the flow of electric current. The first transistor was made in 1947 and they soon replaced electronic valves in radios. At one time all transistors were made separately, but in 1971 they began to be made with thousands of other electronic components on a small slice of silicon no bigger than your finger nail. The result was a complete electronic circuit called an integrated circuit or chip. These are used in calculators, digital watches, computers and video recorders. Today micro-processors, the most advanced chips of all, are used in computers, to run car engines, drive trains and fly aircraft.

Great advances have been made in medicine since the war. In 1947 it was discovered how to mass-produce penicillin, a drug that kills many germs and bacteria. Many useful drugs have been discovered since then, including insulin used to treat diabetic patients.

In the 1950s a vaccine against polio, a disease which crippled children, was discovered. However, not all new drugs are successful. In 1961 a number of children were born with deformities, caused by their mothers taking Thalidomide during pregnancy. Great developments have taken place in the field of surgery since the war. In 1967 the first human heart transplant was carried out. Since then many heart, liver and kidney transplants have been carried out. New technology in medicine has also been developed, including X-ray machines, body scanners and ultrasound scanners which can build up pictures to help doctors check the development of an unborn baby inside its mother's womb.

▶ *A receiving dish on Goonhilly Downs which sends and receives signals to and from satellites and spacecraft.*

▲ *The first artificial satellite was launched by the then USSR in 1957.*

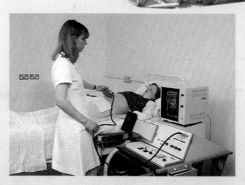

▲ *An ultra-sound scanner can show the baby's development in the mother's womb.*

INDEX